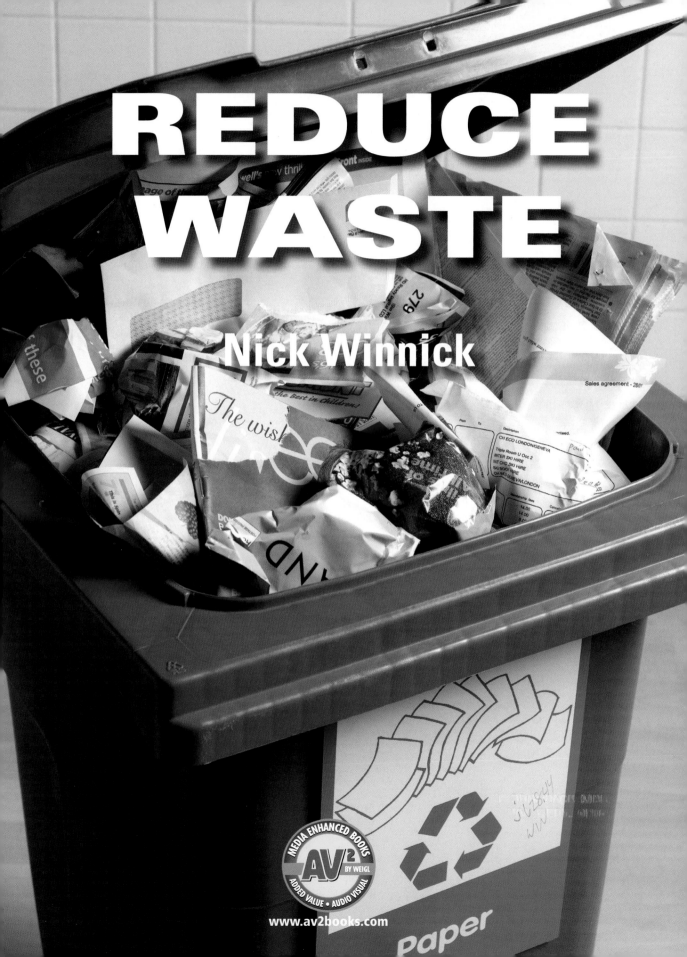

REDUCE WASTE

Nick Winnick

www.av2books.com

Paper

AV² provides enriched content that supplements and complements this book. Weigl's AV² books strive to create inspired learning and engage young minds in a total learning experience.

Your AV² Media Enhanced books come alive with...

Audio
Listen to sections of the book read aloud.

Key Words
Study vocabulary, and complete a matching word activity.

Video
Watch informative video clips.

Quizzes
Test your knowledge.

Embedded Weblinks
Gain additional information for research.

Slide Show
View images and captions, and prepare a presentation.

Go to **www.av2books.com**, and enter this book's unique code.

BOOK CODE

G 254246

AV² by Weigl brings you media enhanced books that support active learning.

Try This!
Complete activities and hands-on experiments.

... and much, much more!

AV² by Weigl
350 5th Avenue, 59th Floor
New York, NY 10118
Web site: www.av2books.com   www.weigl.com

Library of Congress Cataloging-in-Publication Data available upon request.
Fax 1-866-44-WEIGL for the attention of the Publishing Records department.

ISBN 978-1-61690-100-4 (hard cover)
ISBN 978-1-61690-101-1 (soft cover)

Printed in the United States of America in North Mankato, Minnesota
2 3 4 5 6 7 8 9 0 15 14 13 12 11

082011
WEP170811

Project Coordinators: Heather C. Hudak, Robert Famighetti
Design: Terry Paulhus
Project Editor: Emily Dolbear
Photo Research: Edward A. Thomas
Layout and Production: Tammy West

CONTENTS

MAKING THE WORLD A GREENER PLACE

How can you make the world a greener place? You can help the planet by reducing your **carbon footprint**. A carbon footprint is the measure of **greenhouse gases** produced by human activities.

Greenhouse gases are created by burning fossil fuels. People burn fossil fuels for electricity, heating, and powering vehicles. One of the biggest causes of **climate change** is the greenhouse gas known as carbon dioxide. Many scientists believe that carbon emissions are more damaging to Earth than any other kind of pollution.

There are many ways you can reduce your carbon footprint. One way is to walk or ride your bike instead of riding in a car. You can turn off lights when you leave a room to reduce energy waste. Reusing plastic shopping bags to carry other items is another way to help the environment. You can recycle newspaper so that fewer trees are chopped down to make new paper.

HOW CAN YOU REDUCE WASTE?

Reducing waste is one of the easiest ways you can help the environment. Once you decide to reduce the amount of waste you produce, you can learn many different ways to do it. Buying more items than you actually need can lead to excessive waste. Before making purchases, whether you are buying food or a new piece of electronic equipment, consider the waste the purchase will produce. Does the food item have an excessive amount of packaging? If it does have packaging, is that packaging **recyclable** or made from recycled materials? Do you need a new TV, or could you have an old one fixed or buy a used one? These are the types of questions to ask when you and your family are trying to reduce waste.

1 LOOKING TO THE FUTURE

I n the future, the world's population will likely grow much larger than it is today. How can the world support more people, yet still be kinder to the environment? The answer has a great deal to do with reducing waste.

WAYS TO REDUCE WASTE
IN THE FUTURE

Think About People

Currently, there are nearly seven billion people on Earth. The population continues to grow, and every person on the planet produces waste. However, there are many simple ways that each person can cut back on the waste he or she produces.

"This growing mountain of garbage and trash represents not only an attitude of indifference toward valuable natural resources, but also a serious economic and public health problem."

–*Jimmy Carter, former U.S. president*

Be Efficient
Efficient energy products use less energy, but they work as well as, or better than, the items they replace. A good example is energy-efficient light bulbs. These bulbs have become popular because they give off the same amount of light as an **incandescent light bulb**. However, they last longer, use less electricity, and can be recycled.

Make Changes
The power to reduce waste lies in our own hands. Many people have started to make changes to become less wasteful in their everyday lives. These changes can have a ripple effect that benefits the world in many ways. For example, foods with less packaging are often more healthful. The next time you are in a grocery store, think about which foods create the most waste. Another example would be cleaning out a closet. Before throwing away an item, think about whether it could be donated to charity. Can you think of any other choices that create less waste and are beneficial to the planet in other ways?

IDEAS FOR WASTE REDUCTION

Think about all the times that you have heard people refer to the "Three Rs." The three Rs are "Reduce, Reuse, Recycle." Reducing is one of the most important parts of being green.

WAYS TO REDUCE THE WASTE YOU PRODUCE

Think Twice

Before you buy any item, ask yourself whether you really need it. A great deal of waste is created when people buy items they do not need or cannot use. It is a good idea to remember the following phrase whenever you are thinking of buying an item. "Buy what you need, and use what you buy."

"Our personal consumer choices have ecological, social, and spiritual consequences. It is time to re-examine some of our deeply held notions that underlie our lifestyles."
–David Suzuki, biologist and environmentalist

"Precycle"

Another way to reduce waste is to **precycle**. Precycling refers to planning purchases with recycling in mind. For example, you may have a choice between two brands of eggs. They are the same price, but one comes in a Styrofoam container, and the other in a cardboard container. The cardboard can be recycled, and even if it should be thrown out, cardboard is **biodegradable**. The Styrofoam would have to be thrown away. It is not known exactly how long it takes for Styrofoam to break down, but it will last for at least 100 years. The eggs in the cardboard container are the better choice for the environment.

Try a New Activity

Do you spend a great deal of time shopping with your friends? Some people think of shopping as a fun, leisure activity or as a hobby. One result of spending free time shopping may be buying items when you do not really need them. Trying a new activity, such as a sport or gardening, can reduce waste. There is very little waste created by a tomato that you have grown yourself.

3 PUTTING ITEMS TO
NEW USES

Reusing can be thought of as rescuing things that would otherwise be wasted. A water bottle might be recyclable, but it could be refilled and reused instead of buying another bottle of water. If a cell phone or a camera breaks, it may be possible to have it repaired rather than buying a new one.

WAYS TO REUSE ITEMS

Ask Questions

Take a close look at an item you are thinking about throwing away. Maybe it is a bicycle with a broken gear shift or an old shirt that no longer fits. Ask yourself the following questions. "Can I still use this?" and "could someone else use this?" If the answer to either question is "yes," there are many ways you can reuse that item.

Find New Uses

Many **disposable** products can be used multiple times before they are thrown away or recycled. Plastic knives and forks can be washed and re-used for school lunches. Plastic shopping bags can be used as trash can liners or to pick up dog waste. Plastic water or soda bottles

can be refilled and reused. What other items could be used more than once before they are discarded? Every time you re-use an item rather than buying or using something new for the same purpose, you are reducing waste.

Repair or Donate

Repairing a damaged item can often be cheaper than replacing it. If you do not have a family member who knows how to do this, consider calling the store where you purchased the item for advice about having it fixed. Items you can no longer use or that you no longer need can be helpful to others. Many charities, such as Goodwill and the Salvation Army, can make sure that donated clothing and household goods get to people in need. A yard sale is another way to ensure your items continue to be used.

"A society is defined not only by what it creates, but by what it refuses to destroy."

–*John Sawhill, economist and conservationist*

4

REDUCING WASTE BY
RECYCLING

Eventually, even well-made products and materials wear out. When car tires wear down, an old house is demolished, or an aluminum can is emptied, the old item can often be turned into something new. As recycling technology improves, less and less of what we use has to become waste.

WAYS TO RECYCLE MORE WASTE

Find a Recycling Program

Most cities and towns in North America offer recycling programs. These places will accept, sort, and, sometimes, collect recyclable items from their residents. In recent years, more items have become acceptable for recycling. Not long ago, plastic items, such as shampoo bottles, would be sent to **landfills**. Now, many plastic products are often recycled. Most recycling programs will take all types of glass, paper,

and food cans. Look online to find out if there is a recycling program in your area and to see what items the program accepts. You can find this information at **www.epa.gov**.

Spread the Word

Recycling one aluminum can saves enough energy to run a television for three hours. Be a good example for your family and friends. Talk to people about recycling and explain how much it can help Earth's environment. Some people think that recycling takes a great deal of work, but ask them to try it for one week. They will be probably be surprised by how easy it is.

> "What we do today, right now, will have an accumulated effect on all of our tomorrows."
> –Alexandra Stoddard, journalist

Seek Out Recycled Materials

Many of the items used in day-to-day life can be made at least partly from recycled materials. The paper used in many books is made using recycled paper. The asphalt on streets and sidewalks may contain shredded pieces of old tires. Glass can be melted down and formed into new jars and bottles. Many plastics can also be recycled in this way. Before you make a purchase, research the opportunities to buy items made from recycled materials. For example, if you want to buy a new pair of earrings, you can seek out a set made from recycled bottles. Does your family need a mat for the front door? One company offers welcome mats made from old flip flops.

5 PRODUCE LESS FOOD WASTE

Around the world, nearly 30 percent of people's food supply is lost to spoilage or waste. This is a big problem, but it is easy to solve. You can start by reducing food waste in your own kitchen.

WAYS TO REDUCE FOOD WASTE

Plan Ahead

A large amount of food waste is caused by poor planning. Before purchasing a large bag of apples, ask yourself if your family is likely to  use all of them before they spoil. Getting together with your family to plan your grocery shopping can drastically reduce the amount of food that is lost to spoilage.

Think Before You Toss

Imagine you are cleaning out your refrigerator. What can you do with three  strawberries, half an apple, and a carrot? These might not be very satisfying on their own, but blended together with some yogurt, they can make a smoothie. A few vegetables and some leftover chicken can be used to make soup. Carrots and many other vegetables are healthful treats for pets, such as dogs and guinea pigs. Some foods that seem unappetizing are ideal for baking. For example, overripe bananas can be used to make banana bread, and stale bread can be made into bread pudding. If you think creatively, you will find yourself eating well, wasting less food, and saving money on groceries.

"When we see land as a community to which we belong, we may begin to use it with love and respect."

–*Aldo Leopold, ecologist*

Cook More

One of the easiest ways to avoid food waste is to cook more. The leftovers can be used for future meals. Many families have busy schedules and rely on fast food for quick meals. Fast food is quick and convenient, but it comes at a great cost to the environment. Experts estimate that fast food waste makes up 20 percent of all trash. Many cookbooks and cooking websites are devoted to the topic of quick and heathful meals. Sit down with your family, and think about how you could help with meal planning and preparation. Leftovers can be packaged in reusable containers for work and school lunches the next day.

6 PROBLEMS WITH PLASTICS

Items made of plastic create one of the biggest waste problems in the world today. Plastic is inexpensive and easy to produce. Many items made of plastic are durable and do not break easily. However, when something made of plastic is thrown away, it does not break down quickly. Plastic waste stays in landfills for a very long time.

WAYS TO REDUCE PLASTIC WASTE

Bring Your Own Shopping Bags

One of the biggest sources of plastic waste is shopping bags. Between 500 billion and 1 trillion plastic shopping bags are used around the world every year. Most of these bags are not recycled. The bags cause serious problems for fish and other wildlife if they are not disposed of safely. Animals may choke on or be suffocated by discarded plastic bags, for example. Since many kinds of plastic are made mainly from **petroleum**, each ton (metric tons) of plastic shopping bags produced uses the equivalent of 11 barrels of oil. Bringing reusable bags with you to the supermarket every time you shop will reduce the need for plastic shopping bags.

"I now believe plastic debris to be the most common surface feature of the world's oceans. . . . [A] fourth of the planet's surface area has become an accumulator of floating plastic debris."
–Charles Moore, oceanographer

Avoid Plastic Cutlery

Disposable plastic products are a large source of plastic waste. Think about the plastic knives, forks, and straws given away at most fast food restaurants. Each product is used for only a few minutes, but it will sit in a landfill for thousands of years before it breaks down. In contrast, metal utensils can be used thousands of times before they are no longer useful. Carrying a fork and spoon in your backpack can help reduce waste.

Reduce and Recycle

In the northern part of the Pacific Ocean, there is a place called the North Pacific **Gyre**. Here, currents from around the world meet in a swirl of

water the size of the United States. The way these currents flow, anything caught in them tends to drift toward the middle. In the center of this gyre, there is a floating expanse of plastic rubbish twice the size of Texas. People can help keep plastic out of the ocean by being more cautious with their use and disposal of plastic.

7 EFFICIENT ENERGY

Energy from many sources makes our world run. It powers cars, lights homes, and cooks food. Depending on how it is used, energy may be wasted. Wasted energy is one of the easiest problems to solve. New technologies and new ideas are helping to reduce wasted energy. These technologies may also save people money.

WAYS TO MONITOR ENERGY USE

Use Power Strips Did you know that some devices use power whenever they are plugged in, whether they are turned on or not? These energy-sucking devices are sometimes referred to as "vampires." Cell phone chargers, DVD players, microwave ovens, and coffee makers can be "vampires." There are a couple of different ways that you can slay these vampires. The simplest way is to unplug the devices. Many people choose to plug their devices into a power strip or bar. Power strips have several outlets with a single plug. They have switches that can be used to easily cut off power to every device plugged into the strip.

> "Pollution is nothing but the resources we are not harvesting. We allow them to disperse because we've been ignorant of their value."
> –Buckminster Fuller, architect and inventor

Try Kill-A-Watt Many families in the United States have saved money and energy by installing a power meter called a Kill-A-**Watt**. These meters attach to a home's electrical system.

Kill-A-Watt meters display how much energy is being used and how much this energy costs. With this information, many people find it easier to keep track of how much energy they use.

Keep Insulated Think about the difference between hot chocolate in a cup and hot chocolate in a thermos. The liquid in the thermos stays hot longer because the thermos is **insulated**. The same idea is true for homes. In cold weather, well-insulated homes get warm faster and stay warm longer than homes with poor insulation. This means that less energy and less money is needed to heat well-insulated homes. Improving a home's insulation by sealing drafts and properly insulating the roof, walls, and floor, can be one of smartest financial and environmental decisions a family can make.

8 USING LESS
WATER

Earth may be covered by water, but only a small portion of that water is drinkable. Since all humans must drink water to survive, it is important not to waste this resource. Modern homes and businesses can use a great deal of fresh water, and, often, much of this water is wasted. Around the world, people are finding simple and innovative ways to save water.

WAYS TO REDUCE WATER USE

Reuse Graywater

There are three major "types" of water in a modern home. They are drinking water, waste disposal water, and the water used for cooking, bathing, cleaning, and laundry, which is called graywater. Most of the water used in any home will become graywater. Many developers have begun installing graywater treatment systems in homes. Using cleaning chemicals and filters, the graywater is treated until it can be used again for many household purposes. Homes with a graywater system can reduce their water use and their water bill by more than 50 percent. Even without a treatment system, you can reuse some graywater. Try collecting the water that runs in the shower while the water gets hot and then using it to water plants.

Collect Rainwater

Many homes supplement their water intake by collecting rainwater. This can be as simple as draining your home's gutters into a bucket for watering the garden, or as sophisticated as a system that filters and pumps water into the home. Inexpensive rain barrels are available at most hardware stores.

Most of these barrels have a screen that keeps out leaves and other debris. Some even have taps so that watering cans or birdbaths can easily be filled with water from the barrel.

> "When the well is dry, we know the worth of water."
>
> —*Benjamin Franklin, statesman, scientist, inventor, and author*

Modify Toilets

A great deal of the water used in any home is flushed down the toilet. However, there are ways to reduce the amount of water lost down the drain in your home. New low-flush toilets use much less water than older models, and many have an option to flush with more water when needed. If your family does not have a new toilet, you can try this simple trick instead. Open the back tank of your toilet, and place a brick or a sealed container of water in the tank. The toilet will keep the same level of water in the tank without using as much water with each flush.

MAKING COMPOST

Some types of waste can be harder to reduce than others. You cannot add spoiled food or old teabags to a recycling bin. Most families throw this kind of waste into the garbage. It is possible, however, to find a use for many types of spoiled or uneaten food.

WAYS TO USE COMPOST AT HOME

Use Compost Containers

Fungi and **bacteria** can cause food to spoil. Most of the time, this spoiled food is thrown away. However, keeping some types of food in a special container can turn it into **compost**. Most composting is done outdoors. In addition to spoiled food, people put garden trimmings and parts of food that cannot be eaten, such as

cornhusks and eggshells, into a container in their garden. As these materials break down, they turn into a soil-like material that is helpful to plants. Every so often, some of the compost can be removed and used as **fertilizer**. Keep in mind that meat and dairy products cannot be composted.

> "When plants die, they're recycled into basic elements [by organisms in the soil] and become a part of new plants. It's a closed cycle. There is no bio-waste."
> –Alice Friedemann, journalist

Make Compost for Others

Many people do not have gardens, but almost everyone knows someone who does. If you do not have a use for compost at your home, ask your friends and family to see if anyone would like extra compost. Many gardeners would be happy for the help, and

you could use some of your home's waste to make compost for them. Small compost buckets are inexpensive, can be kept in the house or garage, and are easy to transport to the person who will use the compost.

Try Vermiculture

Not everyone can compost outdoors. People who live in apartments, for example, might not have this option. In many cases, people who wish to compost indoors use vermiculture. Vermiculture uses a colony of worms, such as earthworms, to break down food that would otherwise be wasted. Vermiculture can be difficult to use because the worms' **habitat** must be kept at a certain temperature and humidity level. However, the worms produce beneficial fertilizer for plants in small gardens or in window boxes.

10 HELPING YOUR COMMUNITY

Protecting the environment is a big job. Taking individual action is a great start, but a large group will see faster results. Think about ways that you could use what you have learned about reducing waste to help your community.

WAYS TO REDUCE WASTE IN A COMMUNITY

Hold Bottle Drives
In some states, people may receive money for turning in empty bottles and cans for recycling. The payment is 5 or 10 cents per can or bottle, which will add up over time. Bottle drives are a great way to earn money and help the environment. In a bottle drive, people go to homes and businesses in a community and ask residents to donate bottles and cans. Many groups, such as sports teams and charity organizations, use this method to earn money for their activities.

Go Online
The Web can be a great resource for waste reduction. The Freecycle Network is a nonprofit group devoted to exchanging free items and keeping objects out of landfills. Some community sites have free classified sections where people can list items that they no longer need. These items can range from moving boxes to furniture. You can also find sites that list upcoming flea markets and garage sales. If you are interested in pursuing a listing, ask an adult for help.

Pool Resources
One of the greenest ways to help your community is to keep items from being wasted in the first place. Imagine that you have old clothes, books, or sports equipment that you no longer need. You may not have enough to hold a yard sale of your own, but perhaps you can hold one with friends or neighbors. If all of you pool your resources and hold a sale together, you can earn money, provide your friends and neighbors with items they might need, and keep items from being thrown away.

10 Ways to Make Your Home Green

Stop Air Leaks

Heat is lost very quickly through air leaks. Windows, doors, light switches, and electrical outlets may be letting warm air escape. This means that more energy has to be used to heat the house. Sources of heat loss can be sealed with foam, **caulking**, or **weatherstripping**.

Turn It Off

If you do not need it, do not run it. Any room without people in it should not have a light on and should not have electronics running.

Set Your Thermostat

You can save money on heating costs and save energy by lowering your thermostat when you are out of the house or asleep. Hardware stores sell thermostats with timers that can be programmed to change temperatures at pre-set times.

Request the Test

Certified home energy raters can test homes with a "blower door." This device pumps air into your home and helps to find poorly insulated or drafty areas. Finding and fixing these will help your home become more energy efficient.

Look for the ENERGY STAR Logo

When your family is buying a new appliance, look for the ENERGY STAR logo. This logo identifies products that have been certified by the U. S. Environmental Protection Agency to be energy-efficient. Often, these products use 10 to 30 percent less energy than their competitors.

If you are interested in reducing waste, you can start in your home. Here are 10 simple ways to make a home more efficient.

Go With the Low-Flow

Installing low-flow showerheads will save water. These are inexpensive and easy to install, and they can save money on water bills every year.

Use Coiled Fluorescent Light Bulbs (CFLs)

Replacing older incandescent bulbs with CFLs, which are very energy efficient, will reduce your family's electric bill. If everyone in the United States made this change, the reduced need for electricity could mean that more than 5 billion tons (4.5 billion metric tons) of greenhouse gases would not enter the atmosphere.

Clean and Maintain Your Furnace

If your home has a furnace, it is a good idea for your family to have it cleaned every second year. This improves the furnace's efficiency by between 5 and 10 percent. It also reduces heating costs and energy usage.

Plant a Tree

A shade tree or bushes that will grow tall in your front yard can save money on air conditioning in the summer. If your family plants a leafy tree, it will let sunlight through in the winter when its leaves have fallen off, helping to reduce heating costs.

Cover Your Water Heater

Putting an inexpensive insulated cover around your water heater keeps the water hot longer, which can save a great deal of energy. To save money, and reduce the risk of accidental burns, your family can turn your water heater's temperature down a few degrees.

Green Careers

In order to have a clean and healthy world in the future, we need to start working toward it now. These are two of the potential careers for people who are interested in reducing waste.

Green Artist

Career

Green artists combine their love of art with a passion for the environment. These artists may sculpt with recycled materials, create weavings with recycled fibers, design jewelry made from used glass, or find any other way to create art without harming Earth. Some green artists work in fashion design, creating clothing from organic cotton and other natural fabrics. Many green artists use their work to educate others about various environmental issues. Some of these artists work on their own. Others may work at design or retail companies.

Education

A bachelor's degree in fine art will give a solid foundation for many artistic careers.

Green Contractor

Career

Green contractors are builders and tradespeople who specialize in eco-friendly products and technologies. Green contractors install insulation, solar panels, graywater systems, and other technologies designed to make homes more energy efficient and environmentally friendly. These individuals often must learn specialized techniques associated with major construction trades, such as electrical work or plumbing.

Education

All U.S. states require contractors to be licensed. The details of these licenses vary by state, but most licensed contractors must pass a multiple-choice exam.

What have you learned about Reducing Waste?

Are you a waste reduction expert?
Take this quiz to test your knowledge.

1 What is one type of waste that is very harmful to life in the ocean?

2 What is an energy "vampire"?

3 Why is "reduce" such an important component of the environmental "Three Rs"?

4 How does compost help a garden?

5 How much of the world's food supply is lost to spoilage and waste?

6 What is the specific name for water that has been used in cooking, cleaning, or laundry?

7 What is the name for composting with a colony of worms?

8 How can you modify an old toilet to save water?

ANSWERS: 1. Disposable plastics. **2.** A device that consumes power whenever it is plugged in, even if it is turned off. **3.** Nothing can be wasted if it is not used in the first place. **4.** By nourishing plants and creating rich soil. **5.** Nearly 30 percent. **6.** Graywater. **7.** Vermiculture. **8.** By placing a brick or sealed container in the back of the tank

Time to Debate

ISSUE   Should cities fund door-to-door collection of materials for recycling programs?

Most people would agree that reducing waste is a good idea. However, there are many different ways to do so, and these specifics are often topics for heated debate. In the case of reducing waste, debate typically centers around the funding of waste management programs. Should a city's taxpayers, for instance, pay for door-to-door collection of recyclable materials? Should the city save that money and depend on people to drop off recyclable materials on their own?

CONS

1. Door-to-door collection will increase taxes for property owners.
2. There is an additional environmental cost in the form of more large trucks on the city's streets.
3. The bins used for recycling collection are unattractive.

PROS

1. Much less potentially recyclable material will be sent to landfills.
2. Easier participation will encourage more people to take part in local recycling programs.
3. Recyclable collection could be merged with other waste collection activities to save money.

WORDS TO KNOW

bacteria: one-celled organisms that live almost everywhere; some kinds break down organic matter for food

biodegradable: capable of safely breaking down through the natural action of the environment or living things

carbon footprint: an estimate of how much carbon dioxide is put into the atmosphere by the activities of a person or a company or the activities at a place

caulking: a waterproof sealant that can be used to close gaps or leaks

climate change: human-generated changes to the world environment; droughts, forest fires, and severe storms are just a few of the ways this can affect the United States

compost: the decayed remains of organic matter, such as food and yard waste, that can improve soil

disposable: intended to be used briefly and then discarded

fertilizer: material that is spread on or worked into soil to help improve its quality

fungi: organisms that, in many cases, live on plants or in soil and that break down organic matter for food

greenhouse gases: carbon dioxide and other gases in the atmosphere that can contribute to global warming

gyre: a large, rotating system of currents

habitat: the place or environment in which an organism lives and grows

incandescent light bulb: a bulb that produces light when electricity passes through a thin wire; much of the energy used to power this type of bulb is lost as heat

insulated: protected from heat, cold, electricity, or sound by a nonconducting material

landfills: places where waste material is deposited

petroleum: a thick mixture of hydrocarbons that is found beneath Earth's surface; used as a raw material for many products

precycle: to use practices that prevent the creation of waste, such as buying used materials

recyclable: capable of being used again

watt: a unit of measure of electrical power

weatherstripping: narrow strips of material often placed along the edges of doors or windows to prevent drafts and heat loss

INDEX

Log on to www.av2books.com

AV² by Weigl brings you media enhanced books that support active learning. Go to **www.av2books.com**, and enter the special code inside the front cover of this book. You will gain access to enriched and enhanced content that supplements and complements this book. Content includes video, audio, web links, quizzes, a slide show, and activities.

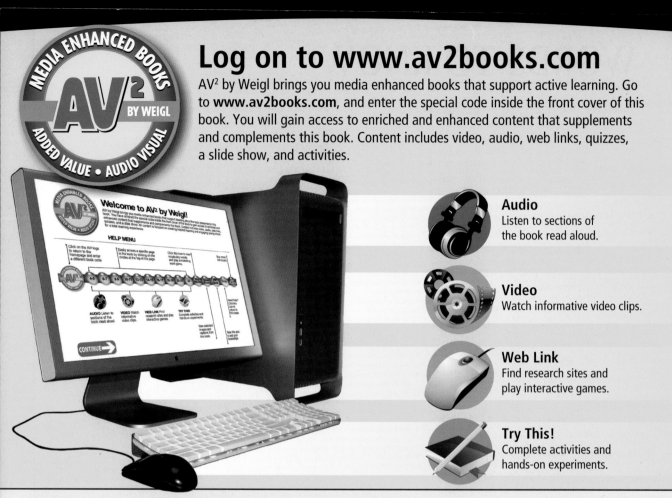

Audio
Listen to sections of the book read aloud.

Video
Watch informative video clips.

Web Link
Find research sites and play interactive games.

Try This!
Complete activities and hands-on experiments.

WHAT'S ONLINE?

Try This! Complete activities and hands-on experiments.	Web Link Find research sites and play interactive games.	Video Watch informative video clips.	EXTRA FEATURES
Pages 12-13 Try this activity about recycling.	**Pages 8-9** Learn more about waste reduction.	**Pages 4-5** Watch a video about reducing waste.	**Audio** Hear introductory audio at the top of every page.
Pages 16-17 Complete an activity about reducing plastic waste.	**Pages 10-11** Link to more information about putting items to new uses.	**Pages 14-15** View a video about food waste.	**Key Words** Study vocabulary, and play a matching word game.
Pages 26-27 Test your knowledge about ways to make your home green.	**Pages 14-15** Find out more about food waste.	**Pages 20-21** Learn more about water use.	**Slide Show** View images and captions, and try a writing activity.
Pages 30 Complete the activity in the book, and then try creating your own debate.	**Pages 28-29** Learn more about green careers.		**AV² Quiz** Take this quiz to test your knowledge